ALLEGL␣ ␣␣

Michael Collins and Winston Churchill: 1921–22
A dramatised account

Mary Kenny

Kildare Street Books
P.O. Box 10073
Dublin 2
Ireland

ALLEGIANCE

Michael Collins and Winston Churchill: 1921–22
A dramatised account

Mary Kenny has been a writer and journalist,
publishing on both sides of the Irish Sea for over
three decades. Her most recent book is a biography
of Lord Haw-Haw, Germany Calling.

For more information see Mary's website:
www.mary-kenny.com

Published in 2005
by Kildare Street Books
P.O. Box 10073 Dublin 2 Ireland

Permission to quote from G.K. Chesterton's Lepanto by arrangement
with A.P. Watt Ltd. on behalf of the Royal Literary Fund,
20 John Street, London WC 1 N 2DR

Performance Rights
Applications for permission to perform this play by
professional or amateur theatre performers, on television, radio
or by schools and colleges to be made by e-mail to:
mary@mary-kenny.com
Or by post to Mary Kenny,
Kildare Street Books,
P.O. Box 10073, Dublin 2, Ireland
Mary Kenny's agent: Louise Greenberg, London

Printed by Ink Communications Ltd.
Unit 38/39, Finglas Business Park,
Tolka Valley Road, Finglas, Dublin 11
website: _www.inkcomm.ie_

Layout and Cover design by Anthony Carey

ISBN 0-9550167-0-3

In memory of Miriam, of London and West Cork,
who became legally Irish just five days before she was taken from us

May perpetual light shine upon her

Contents

Acknowledgements...9

Author's Introduction 11

Allegiance: The Narrative..21

Allegiance: A play in ten scenes...23

Scene One..25

Scene Two..30

Scene Three...36

Scene Four...47

Scene Five..48

Scene Six..59

Scene Seven...78

Scene Eight..80

Scene Nine...85

Scene Ten...86

Appendix I
Churchill and Collins: descriptions of their characters from historical sources,
for the use of actors and students 86

Bibliography..94

Acknowledgements

My thanks to all those who encouraged and made suggestions about this work: my husband, Richard West, first became drawn by the episode of Collins and Churchill as told by William Manchester in *The Last Lion,* and saw, with a veteran reporter's eye, that it was a great story which deserved to be re-explored. My friend Tony Duff first read the play and gave me excellent advice. Max Stafford-Clark was also very kind and encouraging. Thanks to Thomas Griffin of Thurles for his constructive enthusiasm; to Tim Pat Coogan, Bruce Arnold, Seamus Hosey, Mary Rose O'Callaghan and Manus O'Riordan for their helpful and (sometimes critical comments) after a memorable public reading in Dublin, and to Senator Nora Owen, Collins' great-niece, along with Tania Banotti (his great-grand niece) who were so warm and responsive. Thanks most especially to Ronan Wilmot of the New Theatre in Dublin who directed Daniel Riordan and David Murray as Winston and Michael, *Con brio*. My gratitude to my niece Sarah Kenny who was so supportive about the project, and to Ben West for his ideas about playscripts and publishing.

My thanks to those who read the playtext, most notably to Terry Charman at the Imperial War Museum in London, who not only knows everything about Winston Churchill, and everything about the Second World War, but also everything about popular music of the 1920s and 30s. Professor Roy Foster, Carroll Professor of Irish History at Oxford, was also hugely generous and sent me some brilliant Churchilliania of his own.

Tony O'Flaherty of Ink Communications in Dublin printed this text: Tony is a man who brings an exceptional professionalism, care and enthusiasm to his work, and has seen this project as more than a job – but as a production in which he takes pride and interest. Anthony Carey, a most gifted designer whom I much admire, designed the presentation and the logo, as well as editing the text, and I thank them both for bringing this work to publication. *MK*

Mary Kenny is a well-known writer and journalist who publishes on both sides of the Irish Sea. For more information, visit Mary's website: www.mary-kenny.com

Author's Introduction

I wrote this play about the friendship between Michael Collins and Winston Churchill because I felt it was something that had to be written: something pushed me to write it, ever since I came across the description of Michael and Winston's meeting. I also believe that it is a vignette of history which should be more prominently in the public realm, should be considered by those engaged by Irish and Anglo-Irish history, and brought to life through the medium of drama.

I grew up with the legend that Winston Churchill disliked the Irish: that he was "anti-Irish". Churchill was certainly hostile to Irish neutrality during the Second World War, and considered invading the 26 counties of what was then called Éire if the defence of the British realm required it. In turn, many Irish nationalists disliked—even hated—Churchill as the epitome of the British bulldog which had so harshly bullied the Irish nation down the centuries.

Like all legends of history this turns out to be less than nuanced. Things are always more complicated than they seem. And in effect, Winston Churchill had been the midwife to the Irish State as established in 1923.

In researching the story itself, I have drawn on a considerable deposit of biography, history and press reportage relating to Winston Churchill, Michael Collins and the events around the Anglo-Irish Treaty of 1921 and the subsequent foundation of the Irish State. But obviously, the interpretations and some of the fanciful elaboration are my own.

Many historians and biographers refer to the meeting between Churchill and Collins during the Anglo-Irish peace talks which preceded the Treaty, signed in December—Robert Rhodes James, William Manchester and Martin Gilbert among them. Churchill writes about Michael Collins himself in *"The Aftermath"* and in *"Thoughts and Adventures"*—referring specifically to the episode when he pointed out that he, too, had once had a price on his head.

Michael Collins' Irish biographers have played down the Churchill-Collins encounters, possibly because Churchill became generally rather unpopular with Irish nationalists after the Second World War (he did described Eire as "neutral, but skulking"). Both T. Ryle Dwyer and Tim Pat Coogan emphasise the point that Collins didn't trust Churchill, and that he liked Birkenhead best, among the British delegation. Yet Birkenhead himself claimed that Winston and Michael became "fascinated" with one another, and ended up as "bosom friends" (see *Salvidge of Liverpool* in the Bibliography).

Collins didn't *initially* trust Churchill, but he did come to depend upon him, and he did send Winston that fond message of thanks before he died. (See Mary Bromage's careful tracking of the political development of their association.) Churchill also defended Michael Collins and the Free State steadfastly in the House of Commons, against some very rough criticism, and parliamentary extracts quoted in this play are taken from Hansard, the parliamentary record, in 1922.

That Collins and Churchill spent an evening arguing, reciting poetry, and getting rather drunk together is established (and most entertainingly described in William Manchester's *The Last Lion*). Historically, Lord Birkenhead was with Michael and Winston for much of their encounter, but for dramatic reasons, I have distanced him, placing him in a parallel meeting between Lloyd George and Arthur Griffith, which was taking place at the same time.

The play also draws on press reportage in the London press; the media reception given to Collins in particular was extraordinary. Michael had certainly been depicted as a violent gunman (which in some respects, it might be said that he was): but once he arrived at Euston Station for the peace talks, he was treated like a rock star by most of the popular press. The other delegates — both British and Irish — must have been a little bemused, and perhaps envious, that Mick Collins was undoubtedly the celebrity of the whole show. The main exception was the Conservative and Unionist *Morning Post*, and I have drawn upon their sources because these illustrate the bitter opposition which Conservatives and Unionists had to a settlement with the Irish Free State, or even to negotiating with the Sinn

Féin men at all—a significant consideration for a London coalition government which was on the brink of collapsing, as it indeed did.

Moreover, in 1921, the memories of Flanders and the Somme were still all too fresh and I have brought that into the picture, because it is also a key note of the time.

It is a piquant aspect of Anglo-Irish history that Winston Churchill, having previously denounced and disliked Irish rebels—he had a childhood horror of "the Fenians" – came to support and uphold the Irish Free State (militarily too) and Collins' stewardship of it. "Few of the Irishmen who accepted the Treaty," wrote Collins' New Zealand biographer Margery Forester, "can have realised how much they had so far owed to Churchill. He had staked his political fortunes upon it, and had upheld the actions of its Irish signatories in the face of bitter attacks..." It is my interpretation that Churchill saw in Michael Collins the reckless young warrior he had once been: and he sought to teach him, and to help him make that leap from warfare to political leadership. At the time of their meeting, in 1921, Churchill's own political star was on the wane: he believed Michael was the rising political star, within his own firmament.

Winston Churchill never entirely lost that sense of insecurity about an independent and neutral Irish state—he always thought an Ireland which was uncoupled from Britain and the Empire might be a launch-pad for Britain's enemies. This was why he was so concerned about Éire's neutrality in 1939-45. In the light of history, we can now understand that, although it was not a perspective that most Irish people could understand, at all, at the time. They were judging by the light of their history.

All the same, in 1947, as recounted in Roy Foster's indispensable *Paddy and Mr Punch*, Winston had a sort of spiritualist vision of communicating with his father, Lord Randolph Churchill. In this reverie, Lord Randolph asked his son about Ireland: "Did they get Home Rule?" Winston answers: "The South got it, but Ulster stayed with us." "Are the South a Republic?" Winston replies: "No one knows what they are. They are neither in nor out of the Empire. But they are much more friendly to us than they used to be. They have built up a cultured

Roman Catholic system in the South. There has been no anarchy or confusion. They are getting more happy and prosperous. The bitter past is fading." In 1953, when the 26 counties had become a Republic, Winston received De Valera, cordially, in London.

In February 2004, a study published in Dublin suggested that relations between Ireland and Britain were more harmonious than they had ever been in the course of our common history. The matter of "allegiance" had slipped into history for the Irish state — although the question of the Northern Ireland (Winston's "dreary steeples of Fermanagh and Tyrone") remained unsettled, and a continuing source of political trouble, and indeed violence. As Sinn Féin Members of Parliament for Westminster, Gerry Adams and Martin McGuinness still refused to take an oath of allegiance to the British realm, (which has now taken on a new implication in a multi-cultural society.) And yet, overall, it might be said that Winston Churchill's and Michael Collins' common hope has been largely fulfilled — that Ireland be a prosperous nation and that the two islands live in peace and respect.

Winston Churchill
Irish Independant Syndication

Winston Churchill
Irish Independant Syndication

Michael Collins
Irish Independant Syndication

Michael Collins
Irish Independant Syndication

Michael Collins and Arthur Griffith
Irish Independant Syndication

Left to right: Arthur Griffith, Eamonn De Valera, Michael Collins, Harry Boland

Irish Independant Syndication

Allegiance: The narrative

In October 1921, Michael Collins, who had been commander of the IRA in the Irish War of Independence against Great Britain, reluctantly travelled to London as part of a Sinn Féin delegation to negotiate a peace Treaty between Britain and Ireland. This was designed to end hostilities (which the Irish reckoned had lasted 800 years) and to create an Irish State. It attracted a huge amount of interest from home and overseas press and Michael Collins found himself a London celebrity.

Winston Churchill was among the leaders of the British Government delegation negotiating with the six Sinn Féin representatives. The conference encountered many obstacles, most notably the Oath of Allegiance to the King.

Initially, Collins and Churchill regarded each other with suspicion. Yet they gradually became fascinated with each other. One evening, during a difficult phase of negotiations, they got drunk together at Churchill's London home, and ended the evening reciting poetry and singing songs together. Some chord was struck between them which helped to bring the Treaty to fruition. And Winston Churchill, the British Imperialist par excellence thereafter defended the Free State in general and Michael Collins in particular through stormy passages in the House of Commons—when Winston steered the legislation for the Irish Free State through Parliament.

Before Michael Collins died, he sent a message to Churchill: "Tell Winston we could never have done it without him."

This is a dramatised version of how Winston met Michael, and the friendship which developed. Press reports are based on actual newspaper material of the events, and other historical sources are cited in the Appendix. The dialogue—although it draws on statements that Winston Churchill and Michael Collins made—is imagined.

Mary Kenny. Deal and Dublin. 2005
[See also Appendix at end of play text for notes, sources, bibliography.]

ALLEGIANCE.

A play in ten scenes

Characters: Winston Churchill M.P. In his late forties (and late fifties).

Michael Collins. Aged 31.

William Evans, Winston's butler. Twenties/thirties.

Florence Fitzgerald, a reporter for the Daily Express. About 27.

Reginald Morris, a leader-writer for the Morning Post. 40s.

Two London newsboys: one a teenager, another older.

Voices of phone operator. Voices in the House of Commons.

The time: October–December 1921: with retrospectives from 1932

The place: Winston's home at Sussex Gardens, Hyde Park, London.

A telephone booth at the Savoy Hotel.

A small office of the Morning Post newspaper.

A street news vending site.

A visual illusion of the floor and Distinguished Strangers' Gallery of the House of Commons.

Scene One

Music. Suggest "If I had a talking picture of you". Orchestral only.

Winston Churchill is dictating his recollections to a female secretary. Her presence is notional, and may be represented by a silhouette, since she has no words to say: but it was Winston's habit to dictate notes, memoirs, books and even journalism to a secretary, holding in his hand his own hand-written drafts.

We are in the 1930's when Winston is in his late fifties. He is a cherubic-faced man with a balding head, blue eyes, and rounded shoulders. He has a slight lisp which at some moments is more pronounced.

Winston: At the end of 1920, I informed the Prime Minister, Mr. Lloyd George—that I wished to quit the Ministry of War and Air… where I was not regarded as an unqualified success.

Mr. Lloyd George duly rewarded my failures by putting me in charge of…Ireland

Pause.

Winston: *(continuing)* No. By putting me in charge of Ireland, and the Middle East: those two most recalcitrant regions affecting our great British Empire.

But Ireland, I told the Cabinet, could wait. The tortured turbulence in the Middle East required all my attention. And I opposed any consideration of Home Rule for Ireland while the murder gang of Sinn Féiners went unpunished.

The British nation—having come grimly through the slaughter of Armageddon in Flanders and the Somme was not about to be intimidated by the squalid scenes of guerrilla warfare being enacted across the Irish Channel.

Pause. Lights a cigar.

Winston: *(continuing)* But events in Ireland became brutal and exasperating. The Sinn Féiners murdered our forces with impunity.

The Dublin police could not be relied upon to keep the King's Peace. We were obliged to send auxiliary military forces who were swiftly designated, "the Black and Tans"—entirely for sartorial reasons.

Backdrop pictures of Black and Tans.

Winston: *(continuing)* Notwithstanding our endeavours, the Sinn Féiners continued to inflict grave damage on the Crown Forces. And set about assassinating many innocent bystanders whom they chose to describe as "spies".

An elderly lady in County Cork, a Mrs. Lindsey, was liquidated by the Sinn Féiners merely because she had correctly informed the authorities about breaches of the law.

It was, I told my colleagues in Cabinet, quite monstrous that we had some *two hundred murders* and so few hangings in just retribution.

Pause.

We had successfully imposed the death penalty on a young IRA medical student, one Kevin Barry—who had attacked and killed three of our young soldiers.

Backdrop picture of Kevin Barry.

Winston: *(continuing)* But the Irish orchestrated a melodrama—of considerable theatrical energy at the time of his execution.

Background noise of crowd.

As the young man mounted the scaffold, a crowd of 5,000 people recited prayers and sang hymns at Mountjoy Jail, that Monday morning.

Faint musical sound of the ballad of Kevin Barry.

Pause. He walks up and down, notes in hand.

Winston: *(continuing)* Our timing was not sagacious.

Five days previously, the Mayor of Cork, Terence MacSwiney, had succumbed after a hunger strike against our policies. His demise had excited much clamour throughout the Empire. Neither was it prudent to send Kevin Barry to the gallows on All Saints Day, when every church bell in Ireland tolled.

Disraeli once described the Irish as — "sunk in clannish brawls and coarse idolatry."

Pause.

Winston: *(continuing)* I see this meets with your disapproval, Dorothea!

Very well: you may erase the allusion to Mr. Disraeli's outburst. Your tender feminine heart is wary of offending feelings!

But continue…Our intelligence services informed us that Mr. Michael Collins had arranged to place explosives in Mountjoy Jail to rescue his man; but drew back from the strategy because of the difficulty of its execution.

Pause with chuckle.

Because of the difficulty of carrying out the escape.

Pause.

My wife, Clementine had always taken a more lenient view of the Irish question: more lenient than those of us burdened with the responsibility of office. She concurred that the Irish murders were very terrible. Yet she counselled a conciliatory approach… In the summer of 1921 she exhorted me to strive for moderation and justice in Ireland.

"I should", she said, "put myself in the place of the Irish". But I have never put myself in the place of any other nation or people! My purpose is to defend the interests of Great Britain.

More artfully, she then observed that I would never be cowed or intimidated by repression or reprisals. Why should I expect the Sinn Féin leaders to be any different in their response?

Pause.

Winston: *(continuing)* My darling Clementine then said quite the worst thing of all. She said my attitude was Hunnish.

Hunnish! Hah!

He takes up a glass of whisky. Change of mood from indignant to sorrowful.

But in truth, the sorrows that touched me in that summer of 1921 may have worked some alchemy of change in me. And my views about Ireland were, in parallel, altering. The iron fist had not brought success. We must henceforth essay something of the velvet glove.

Pause

I informed the Prime Minister, Mr. David Lloyd George, that I would support him in a Truce with the rebels. And that we should proceed with negotiations that would bring an end to the long conflict between England and Ireland.

Paces up and down.

The Irish leader, Mr. De Valera, *(he pronounces it Dee Valera)* parleyed with Lloyd George in that summer of 1921—when my personal sorrows were at full tide…

But De Valera declined to attend the October peace conference himself. He sent, in his stead, men considered to be far more dangerous than he.

A pause.

Winston: *(Now very ponderous and dramatic)*

To receive such men as these—in formal negotiations—must be regarded as one of the most questionable and hazardous experiments upon which a great empire—in the plenitude of its power, and on the morrow of its greatest victory—could ever have embarked.

Long pause. Suggest back projection photographs of Irish delegation.

Winston: *(continuing)* The Irish delegation was led by Mr. Arthur Griffith.

In the earlier years of the century he had advocated that Great Britain and Ireland should be joined together as were the dual monarchies of Austria-Hungary.

Mr. Griffith was that most unusual phenomenon: a taciturn Irishman. He spoke little. Moreover, he was not in robust health, and in consequence, the leadership of the delegation passed, in effect, to Mr. Michael Collins.

Solemn pause.

Now Mr. Collins was, by this time, a legend among the gunmen and revolutionaries who held so much of Ireland in thrall.

His prestige and influence amongst all extremists was high.

He stood far nearer to the terrible incidents of the conflict than any other man among that delegation.

Backdrop picture of Michael Collins

Winston: Collins had become a prodigy of our popular press: an admixture of the Mask of Zorro, of Zapata the Mexican, and Dick Turpin, the Highway Felon.

And this was the personage who was to be the chief negotiator in our proposed settlement for an Irish State.

After eight centuries of unhappy relations between the sister nations of England and Ireland...

Winston looks thoughtfully into the distance as the scene fades.

Darkness to indicate a passage of time...

Scene Two

A split stage. Exaggeratedly bright popular music of early 1920s period, with strong dance flavour. Suggest a band version of "Ain't we got fun?"

Lights up reveal, first, Florence Fitzgerald striding towards a telephone booth in the Savoy Hotel, London. She is dressed in the full flapper style of the 1920s. She is a confident young woman of Anglo-Irish background who is something of a star reporter on the Daily Express—at this time a popular mainstream newspaper with a reputation for news scoops.

Operator's voice: Just putting you through…

Clicking sounds.

Florence: Hello—it's Florence Fitzgerald here!
I am telephoning from the Savoy Hotel—that's Temple Bar 1234, in case we're cut off.

Pause.

Hey-ho! It's yourself, Harry! How are you at all? *Pause.*

Oh… parties, parties, parties. Yes, London is well and truly back to life after all that ghastly war depression!

Florence is speaking to the copytaker at the newspaper—who she often speaks to—and who will transcribe to a typewriter, at virtually, but not quite, normal talking speed, her report. Pauses for his responses and interjections.

Oh, yes—plenty of flappers behaving badly at the Café Royal! Oh, they're not interested in the vote, Harry. Ah, but you'll like this one, old bean. I'm now reporting the sensational Irish Peace Conference.

Pause.

Oh yes, big stuff. The whole of London wants to know about Michael Collins. *Pause.* Yes, he is rather handsome—*(Sarcastic)* My girlish heart's a-flutter! All right—are we ready to go?

Florence opens her mouth to begin her report: lights down on Florence and lights up on other side of stage to reveal a man standing at a lectern, examining a newspaper galley proof. He is Reginald Morris, the chief leader-writer for the Morning Post, a diehard Conservative and Unionist newspaper. He is in shirt-sleeves, and braces. He is reading his proof aloud, with an upper-class accent just tinged with Northern Ireland overtones.

Reginald: Header: Lloyd George shakes hands with Murder!

He begins in a normal voice, but becomes vehement and bitter

> No more degrading or ignominious posture defiles the annals of the British nation — than that which the British Government assumed when it "shook hands with murder". When it shook hands "cordially", bandied gossip and cigars, and entered into negotiations with the chosen spokesmen of the foulest gang of liars and assassins that ever cheated the hangman's noose. *(Emphasis)*

As he speaks, suggest backdrop of Orangemen.

> Those of us who rejoice in the description "loyalist" find it difficult indeed to be loyal — to a Britain which has cringed to murder: whose mouth, stopped with the filth of the political dung heap, has uttered no protest at this spectacle.
>
> Is this, we ask, as Michael Collins and Robert Barton — murderers and instigators of murders — ride up Whitehall flanked by their pistoleers,...

Pause as he makes some marks on the text.

Reginald: *(continuing)* ...to grasp the hand of the dishonoured Prime Minister of England...is this, we ask, the same British people whose souls went up to God from the threshing floor in Flanders and Gallipoli, that the Prussian brute might not set his heel upon the world?

Breaking off from text to murmur to himself.

> By God, that'll show them! That'll show them what British Loyalists think — of His Majesty's government shaking hands with murder!

Fade on Reginald. Return to Florence.

Florence: *(Very bright and jolly)* Paragraph: initial cap: Euston Station was thronged with many thousands of people — mainly, but not altogether, Irish Londoners — for the arrival of Mr. Michael Collins and his entourage for the Irish Peace conference.

Seldom have we witnessed such scenes of wild popular acclamation than those which greeted Michael Collins as he alighted from the Irish Mailboat train travelling from Kingstown and Holyhead.

Florence: *(continuing)* A roar of joy and applause arose — like a seaswell — to the arches of Euston Station. When the crowd glimpsed Mr. Collins, dressed in greatcoat and Trilby hat.

We might have been in the presence of Mr. Rudolf Valentino or Mr. Charlie Chaplin: or some other idol from the silver screen. He stilled the crowd with a single wave of his hand.

"We come with good will in our hearts and hopes of success" he said. Quote, unquote. "If Mr. Lloyd George, Mr. Winston Churchill and the rest of the British Cabinet will meet us in the same spirit — I am not without hope that we shall not have come here in vain."

Noise of cheering crowds.

Florence takes out a cigarette holder and places a cigarette in it.

Florence: *(continuing)* Mr. Collins and the Irish delegation have come to London for a conference fraught with the gravest consequence for the Empire.

Seldom, since the funeral of Kind Edward the Seventh, have we seen such a crowd of reporters and press men descend upon London from all over the Empire, and the United States.

The Prime Minister, Mr. Lloyd George, with Mr. Winston Churchill M.P. will meet the six Sinn Féin deputies.

Shall I spell, Sinn Féin, Harry? S as in Sugar, I as in Iris, N as in November — you've got it. Yes. You know it, of course. Yes. You told me your cousin in Cork was shot by the rebels because he fought for the King in Flanders.

Florence: *(continuing)* But things are changing, Harry. You'll see big changes in Ireland soon…Continue text: these Sinn Féin delegates will settle, with the Crown, the Irish demand for self-government. Much is hoped from this conference. But much has to be overcome.

Fade on Florence. Lights up on Reginald.

Reginald: *(after another pause)* The Irish hate England with a hatred that a hundred years of republicanism will not quench. And they are rejoicing openly today; not just because their Murder Gang is victorious — but because they know that surrender to murder in Ireland, will be followed by surrender to murder in India, in Egypt, in any British Colony or Possession, throughout the turbulent Middle East — and where murder chooses to assert itself.

Irish terrorists have led the way, and terror will follow against all the imperial powers throughout the world!

(Thumps the lectern with passion)

Sinn Féin is rejoicing today not just because it has brought the British Cabinet to its knees. It is rejoicing because it has given England the coward's blow — and the blow has not been returned.

Pause.

Reginald: *(continuing — in a paroxysm of anger)* For this is not the England to which we have sworn loyalty in our own blood — this is the England of the Manchester Guardian and Ramsey Macdonald: the England that pampered the cowardly pacifist and capitulated to the Bolsheviks leading the South Wales miners. And then shook hands with the Irish backstabbers of 1916! The England of the eely Lloyd George and his poltroon colleagues who fear for their own skins! Who fear that Michael Collins and his pistoleers might administer the medicine of terrorism to ***them!*** For this the men of Ulster lost their lives on the bloodied trenches of the Somme!

And all this, within sight of the Cenotaph, within earshot — if the dead hear!

Lights down on Reginald: lights up on Florence, still reporting over the phone.

Florence: Mr. Collins, the Sinn Féin mystery man, has proved as elusive, in London, as he was in Ireland, when a price of a thousand pounds was set on his head...

Pause.

Florence: Official sources say a thousand, Harry. You say five thousand? Good God, man — that's enough to purchase four houses. In Park Lane!

Suggest here large backdrop photographs of Michael Collins and Arthur Griffith arriving at Downing Street. Noise of cheering crowds.

Florence: *(continuing)* Yet when it was known that he was to appear at the Prime Minister's residence, great crowds of people assembled at the entrance to Downing Street to observe the arrival of the delegates to the conference — but especially to catch a glimpse of Michael Collins.

Sir Hamar Greenwood, the Canadian Liberal lawyer, now chief secretary for Ireland was first to be there. Sir Laming Worthington Evans, and Sir Gordon Stewart, the Attorney General were next arrivals.

Pause.

Florence: *(continuing)* Mr. Winston Churchill, Colonial Secretary, came to Number 10 just before eleven o'clock, smiling cheerfully beneath his top hat.

But when the Sinn Féin delegates drove up, there were scenes of wild enthusiasm from the crowd *(Sound of a rousing cheer from crowds)* Mr. Collins made an attempt to evade the photographers by rushing out of the car and through the door to Number 10 Downing Street. His dashing appearance and youthful demeanour made a fabulous impression on the onlookers...

Pause to allow copytaker catch up.

Florence: *(continuing)* The British delegates were made aware, in no uncertain terms, that Michael Collins was the star of this West End show!

Brief pause.

Florence: *(continuing)* Mr. Collins was with Mr. Arthur Griffith, and they were followed by the other Sinn Féin delegates: Mr. Robert Barton, Mr. Gavan Duffy, Mr. Erskine Childers, Mr. Eamonn Duggan. The last of the British delegates arrived after 11 o'clock, the Lord Chancellor, Lord Birkenhead driving up to Number 10 in his own motor car. *(Pause.)*

Standing near the barrier at the entrance to Downing Street was a woman who held aloft a silk banner bearing the words—"Queen of the Rosary, Pray for Us."

Florence: *(breaking off report to speak to the copytaker)* Sweet, isn't it? The Irish and their rosaries! *(resumes reportage…)*

And so the great Anglo-Irish peace conference commences which officials hope will bring a final peace between Britain and Ireland. Ends.

Fade on Florence, taking a drag on a cigarette. Lights up again on Reginald.

Reginald: *(looking very pale and intense)* If the dead could speak, the dead would say: "We fought to save the good name of England and set it among the stars… but you have trodden it into the muck—and we are dishonoured by the shameful compact that England has entered into with the Irish murderers."

He ends on a dramatic pitch. Then his voice becomes very quiet.

Reginald: But Ulster will fight; again and yet again; and Ulster will be right!

Scene fades. Very quiet, echoing resonance of Lillibullero

Following the end of Scene Two, an empty stage, with silhouettes coming and going against a backdrop of Downing Street, to indicate negotiations in progress.

Scene Three

Winston is now in the library of his own home in Sussex Gardens, near Hyde Park, in the winter of 1921. He will have dropped ten years in appearance: he is nearly 48.

We should have an impression of a well-appointed, late-Victorian room, comfortable, cultivated and pleasant, yet a bit of a jumble: the Churchills have not long moved in. There are a great many books; there are several stray children's toys; there is also a well-laden drinks table, and a collection of model soldiers, for Winston's use.

He is seen playing with these model soldiers and his expression is somewhat despondent as he does so. A large glass of whisky is on hand. A manservant, William Evans, appears at the door. He is a very watchful Welshman who takes in everything, and for whom the safety and comfort of Winston Churchill are a professional and even personal priority.

Evans: Mr. Churchill, Mr. Michael Collins is here to see you.

Winston: Thank you, William. I was hoping he might appear. Show him up.

Winston continues playing with his toy soldiers, and does not turn around initially when Michael appears at the door. Michael Collins is an exceptionally striking young man, aged 31, with a rich head of hair, and smartly dressed in a three-piece suit. His demeanour gives an impression of suppressed energy and he is frequently restless. His Cork accent becomes more 'strong and singing' when he is speaking vehemently. He is impressed by the books in the room, but is determined not to be over-awed.

Winston: You are welcome, Mr. Collins, into the den of the lion.

Michael: If you're playing out the Battle of Waterloo, Mr. Churchill, don't forget that the English didn't win the day.
It was won for ye by the Prussian, General Blücher.

Winston: *(Quoting Wellington)* "and a damned, close-run thing", too. *(Turning around)* No, Mr. Collins, this is not the Battle of Waterloo. This is a battle led by one of my ancestors, the Duke of Marlborough, in which victory was ours without the assistance of any damned German.

Michael: Tis well for you to have such illustrious ancestors…

Winston: Your own, no doubt, were being oppressed by the beastly English at the time.

Michael: No doubt about it whatsoever!

Winston: Allow me to offer you some refreshment. *(Rings for Evans, who re-appears very quickly)* What would you care for, Mr. Collins?

Michael: A cup of tea would be grand.

Winston: A pot of tea for one, William.

Michael: Oh, and, William—if you had a bit of cake, or maybe a cream bun?—I wouldn't say no.

Evans: I shall fetch a pot of tea, Mr. Churchill. And I shall enquire about the availability of…cream buns. *(He gives Michael an intense look, assessing the celebrated gunman, and disappears)*

Michael: He thinks I should look the part of a wild Irish gunman.

Winston: *(still fiddling about with the soldiers as a distraction strategy)* The average Englishman is scarcely to be reproved for his opinion of events in Ireland. He has read of many great atrocities.

Michael: *(suspecting Evans to be a policeman in disguise)* I'd say William isn' exactly an average Englishman.

Winston: Well, no, of course — he's Welsh. But he is a sound Britisher!

Michael: I'd say he's also acquainted with your constabulary. I'm very good a identifying policemen.

Winston: We became acutely aware of that, Mr. Collins.

Michael: The joke is now that I'm being protected by your police. They're everywhere I go. But, sure, I suppose I need the protection now. I see the Morning Post has me described as an agent of Bolshevism.

Winston: Au contraire, Mr. Collins, most of the popular press seems to have arrived at the conclusion that you are in the category of a romantic folk hero.

Michael: Arrah, the popular press! They publish a lot of lousey nonsense Sure — as you say — there were nothing but "atrocity" stories a few months ago.

Winston: I am a journalist myself, Mr. Collins. I am aware of the inexactitude: which prevail in the public prints.

Michael: They wrote a lot of one-sided baloney about the Irish "outrages" against the Black and Tans—whom *you* sent to Ireland Mr. Churchill—yourself and Sir Hamer Greenwood.. who—dammit—I also have to sit with, across the negotiating table!

Winston: I did not dispatch the "Black and Tans" to Ireland. *(Pause)* I merely germinated the concept of an Auxiliary Police Force.

Michael: Faith and the Auxies were worse!

Winston: In 1920, we were obliged to recruit an especial militia to prevent Ireland from falling into anarchy and lawlessness.

Michael: Sure, they created anarchy and lawlessness! They went roaring around the country terrorising women and children. They even cut out the tongues of civilians. You didn't read about that in the "Illustrated London News"—did you? Oh, no, it was all "Sinn Féin Outrages"!

And they were drunk, too. *(Wagging his finger)* Mr. Churchill: not one of my men was ever drunk on duty. Not one!

Winston: Our auxiliary troops were acting just as the New York or Chicago police must do with criminal gangs. Your brother is a Chicago policeman...

Michael: Oh, you've checked up on me and my family all right! British spies always on the job!

Winston: Your brother Patrick will enlighten you on the difficulties of dealing with crime and lawlessness. We were faced with assassinations in broad daylight, on the streets of Dublin!

Michael: *(Makes to go)* Look: you ask me to come round to your home and see you privately so that we can talk together... but there's no fucking point in me being here at all, if we are so completely at cross-purposes that we can't even agree on terms of reference: or see eye-to-eye about the roots of the problem!

Our 'lawlessness' was the only way we could affirm the democratic will of our people *(thumping a nearby table)* which was expressed time and time and time again in *your* Parliament...for an independent Ireland.

Do you understand the concept of democracy, Mr. Churchill?

Winston: And there's no damnable advantage in your flying into a temper because your feelings have been offended!

You are a revolutionary learning to be a politician, Mr. Collins, not a swooning maiden with a distaste for robust opinions.

Michael: My feelings aren't offended! My sense of history is offended!

Winston: I speak as an Englishman. And I'm entitled to speak as an Englishman. As you are entitled to speak as an Irishman — and I will do you the honour of listening to you. I asked you to come here to discourse man to man: and that means candour about the way we see things. We will see things differently. But we can still establish some form of trust.

Michael stands silently, his feet apart, containing his simmering feelings.

Winston: *(continuing)* We have met at the conference table with our confrères. We know there are many obstructions and difficulties. Matters are not proceeding as well as we might have hoped — as you yourself hoped on the glad day of your arrival in London.

But we meet to speak our minds, as Englishmen and Irishmen, and we must give expression to our sentiments with honest endeavour.

Silence for a moment.

Michael: Look: I had, and have, no desire whatsoever to be in London for these negotiations! I protested vehemently against the assignment. To come here and negotiate with the British Cabinet was to me a loathsome task! *(Pause. He is upset)*

But I came in the spirit of a soldier who acts against his judgement at the orders of a superior officer. You can surely understand that.

Winston affirms with a nod.

Michael: *(continuing)* And I came here this evening *because you invited me* to speak to you, as an Irishman to an Englishman, so we might be able to make headway in these talks.

Michael: *(continuing)* But you will not lecture me, patronise me, or recite a whole load of bollocks about bringing law and order to Ireland! When all you ever brought was misery and wretchedness!

Michael sits down again in his chair, with a sullen air of duty. Winston goes over to his cigar box.

Winston: Would you care for a cigar, Mr. Collins? I have always found that a superior Havana brightens up any man's "loathsome task".

Michael: *(Bursting out laughing at Winston's grandiosity)* Jesus Christ Almighty —you're in a different world altogether!

(He takes a packet of Three Castles cigarettes from his pocket and leaves it on a table in front of him.)

Tis far from Havana cigars I was reared… I'll smoke a cigarette if I feel the need. Though it's a habit *I can* control, just like any other habit.

Winston: You have a long life before you, to discover the pleasure of a *Romeo y Julietta*. *(Holds up the cigar)* Rolled on the thigh of a young Cuban maiden: I have made it a point of necessity never to be without.

Michael is bemused, against his volition. He doesn't light up as yet. Winston begins fussing with his cigar. Evans reappears with the tea, and two delicate fingers of cake. Over the course of the following conversation, Evans pours the tea. Michael piles three large lumps of sugar into the cup and wolfs the tiny cake pieces in one gulp, looking at them contemptuously. Evans also refills Winston's whisky glass.

Winston: Thank you, William.

Michael: Next time himself has me round here, William —stock in a couple of decent cream buns, will you? This is a class of cake for… little genteel ladies!

Winston: I trust you are comfortable in your London accommodation?

Michael shrugs indifferently.

Winston: I understand you chose not to lodge with the other delegates in the Belgravia neighbourhood.

Michael: Do you know that someone scrawled the words "Collins the Murderer" on the footpath outside Hans Place?

Winston: And do you feel that epithet is distasteful, Mr. Collins?

Michael: Distasteful, my arse. I don't want my whereabouts advertised in that way. I don't care what they call me. You know, you've probably killed more men, or been responsible for more men's deaths than I have. You've been a soldier. You've been in the Boer War. You've sent men to their death at Gallipoli. You hanged Kevin Barry! You had the power of execution many times over.

Winston: *(huffy, because he is notoriously sensitive about Gallipoli and the Dardenelles)* I did not personally execute young Mr. Barry. I participated in a Cabinet meeting which decided against his reprieve. We had to defend the Crown.

Michael: And is everything acceptable in the name of defending the Crown?

Winston: Is everything acceptable in the name of the Irish Republic? Is any innocent Protestant who opposes the Irish Republic to be shot as a so-called "spy"?

I have been a soldier and a commander of men, Mr. Collins. But as soldiers, when we shoot, we wear uniform. There is a chivalric code of conduct for the engagement of war which is not observed by the hidden sniper, the assassin who appears out of nowhere, and as quickly melts into the crowd.

Michael: *(aroused)* The code you're speaking about is the one that is devised by the powerful against the powerless.

Winston: It was devised by the traditions of Christian chivalry.

Michael: Look: in 1916, the British had a garrison of, probably, 40,000 troops, plus a thousand members of the Royal Irish Constabulary. In Dublin alone, the British garrison numbered about 10,000. We were probably—something between 700 and 900 Volunteers.

There's feck-all chivalric code there. It was a peasant nation against a great Empire—and yet, we took on a great Empire! And we brought it to the negotiating table!

There is a brief silence while Winston puffs.

Winston: *(dreamily)* What a great destiny Ireland could have had—and could yet have—as a nation within that family of the British Empire…

Michael: *(Pacing about)* And this is the crux of the matter! These are the obstructions we cannot get over at the conference table…

Arthur Griffith and I are sent here to negotiate an independent Ireland. The people of Ireland have *voted* for independence! And we've fought for it! Aye, we've killed for it, too. It is a miserable and anguishing business to take a human life: it is. *You* should know that…

Winston: The people of the North-East of Ireland have not so voted, Mr. Collins. And you have among you many Southern Unionists who have suffered gravely in these Troubles, and who have been terrorised out of their homes.

Michael: Harmless Catholic families in Belfast have been terrorised this long time! You know well that the Ulster Unionists have tried to wreck Home Rule since 1886.

Michael: *(continuing)* Come on, man—they were stirred up by your own father! "Ulster will fight and Ulster will be right!" "Play the Orange card!" All that fucking nonsense!

Winston: The Ulster Unionists do not require to be stirred up by anyone. They are perfectly capable of stirring up themselves.

And it remains the case that you cannot coerce the North-East of Ireland into your "independent" Ireland, when they quite doggedly resist it. These are the realities of power, Mr. Collins. You will have a Civil War on your hands that would last fifty years.

Michael: *(gloomy)* Christ knows we may have one anyway.

Winston: That will depend on the political skills of all concerned. These political skills are now your responsibility—yours, and others...

Michael: If we cannot coerce *them,* the North-East of Ireland cannot coerce *us,* either—to remain under the Crown.

I mean, talk about lawlessness! Sure, they're the most lawless crowd out—when their own interests are threatened. They were gun-running back in 1913. They were setting up a Provisional Government in defiance of the Crown...

Winston: *(Reflective: conciliatory)* Mr. Collins, I know all this.

I have been a supporter of moderate Home Rule for some years—*moderate* Home Rule, not rebellion—and I have been pelted with rotten fish, in Belfast, for my pains.

But Ulster came to our aid in the Great War, and the young Ulstermen lost their lives in hundreds of thousands on the Somme. They stood by us, when the Southern Irish stabbed us in the back. *(Holding up his hand to prevent Michael's protests)* I am speaking, frankly, as an Englishman: this is the way we see it.

Michael reaches for his cigarettes and lights one.

Michael: Excuse me, Mr. Churchill—but a hundred thousand Irishmen, as near as, fought for the British Army in the Great War, and the majority of them were Southern Catholics! And *they* believed there would be self-government in Ireland as a reward!

Winston: *(continuing his own line of thinking)* Nevertheless, my opinions about Ireland are not a fixed matter.

Michael: Any more than your party allegiance is a fixed matter, maybe?

Winston: I seek to learn by the political process. One strives to hold to certain principles. But one must also learn by experience. I spoke in the House of Commons but a month ago conceding that Ireland's zeal for nationhood must compel respect. And I suggested something that I believe may be considered as a reasonable compromise: that Ireland should attain the status of a Dominion, on a par with Canada, Australia or South Africa. A generous concept, I think.

Michael: Arrah—still the old Imperialism!

Winston: I *am* an Imperialist, and proud to be so. The British Empire has been one of the great civilising missions in history!

Michael: Except in Ireland!

Winston: *(romantically)* The British Empire has represented the rule of law in every clime, under palm and pine.

Michael: Except in Ireland!

Winston: British rule has meant religious tolerance, decent compromise, respect for others, prosperity, freedom, peace, parliamentary democracy…

Michael: Except in Ireland!

Pause.

Winston: I am forming the distinct impression that you do not value the proposal of becoming a Dominion within the Empire.

Michael: Tisn't what our patriots died for. It isn't what I fought for, and risked my life and my men's lives for… "A dominion once again."

Winston: *(walking about, cogitating)* Mr. De Valera's insistence on an Irish Republic can *never* be contemplated by the United Kingdom, Mr. Collins. A separate, foreign Republic of Ireland is out of the question.

It would be a major threat to security on our Western flank. An independent Irish Republic would mean that every Irishman in the British Empire would become an alien enemy.

Michael listens to this sceptically

An independent Irish Republic, which owed no allegiance to the Crown, could forge a dangerous alliance with an enemy of the Realm: with a revived Germany: with Bolshevist Russia, God forfend.

No: we *must* have an oath of allegiance—for our safety and security.

Michael: Allegiance! Another bloody old version of the Orange card!

Music. Suggest "Lillibullero". Fade this scene.

Scene Four

Two London newsboys are seen on stage: one is a teenager dressed in the clothing of poverty but he has the cheeky spirit of the Cockney. One is an older man, possibly a WW I veteran with some war injury. Both are carrying a bag full of newspapers and shout their wares.

Newsboy: Standard, News and Star! Read awl abaut it!

Irish Peace Conference in danger! Mr. Collins mobbed and kissed by crowd of girls at the Albert 'All!

Older newsman: Daily Telegraph, Morning Post! "No surrender for Ulster's rights!" says Craig. "Ulster will fight"—statement from Carson!

Newsboy: Manchester Guardian, Daily Worker! New chance for Irish peace! Diehards in retreat!

Older newsman: Worst fog in London's History…Betrothal of Princess Mary to Lord Lascelles. Irish situation more gloomy.

They exit, shouting their wares: "Standard, News and Star!" "Daily Telegraph, Morning Post." "Manchester Guardian",

"The Times…"…and with various cries of "Latest on Irish Peace Conference!" "De Valera telegrams the Pope!"

"Ulster says No!" "Mr. Collins pictured with Lady Lavery…"

And fading…

Music. "Ain't We Got Fun?"

Scene Five

We return to Winston and Michael. Michael is lighting another cigarette, as though to control his instinct to fight.

Winston: I spent some of my childhood in Ireland, you know. I do know one or two things about the Érin Go Bragh. *(He pronounces it badly)*

And one of them is that you in the South of Ireland, underestimate the complexities of the situation in Ulster. The Ulsterman's feelings, Mr. Collins, run high, and they run deep. If that is not an oxymoron.

Michael: Hah!—even that statement is a rigmarole of English dishonesty! "Ulster" is our ancient province of Ulster, with nine counties: not the truncated Statelet that's now being proposed of *six* counties, just to accommodate the Northern Unionists.

That's what's so bloody dishonest about the whole thing. "Ulster" is not even a province, it's a particular bit carved out of a province, to give the Unionists a permanent majority!

Winston: And what do you think is behind this notion, Mr. Collins?

Michael: Could it just be British Imperialism?

Winston: Real politics, Mr. Collins! Real politics.

Sir James Craig and his Unionists colleagues could bring down this Lloyd George Coalition—with the support of the Tory diehards. They've already threatened to do so. And with a diehard Tory Government, put into power by the Ulster Unionists, you would obtain *nothing at all!*

Michael: We'd fight them, just as we've fought you.

Winston: Do you think the people of Ireland have the appetite to return to the dolorous war conditions of the past two years? Your own Roman Catholic hierarchy has pressed you, from Maynooth itself, for a moderate settlement of peace.

Michael: Oh, fuck the hierarchy! For two pins, I'd have had the Bishop of Cork shot for excommunicating the Sinn Féiners in his diocese. Bishops always side with the prevailing power. All that stuff from St. Paul about the "rightful authority"…

Winston: You sound perilously close to the Orangemen, Mr. Collins! To hell with the Pope! *(Michael throws a cushion across the room in frustration)* This, I think, is not Mr. De Valera's outlook. He regards the Holy Father as his personal amigo. Mr. De Valera is one of your obstructions.

Michael: Leave Dev out of it. He's a decent man, and a fine patriot.

He is smoking, looking out of the window on the park.

Winston: Well: you and I must—just as Mr. Griffith and the Prime Minister must do—we must parley together until we arrive at an understanding of what the British can offer, and what the Irish can accept.

But first, will you perhaps accept a glass of whiskey? Or brandy?

Michael reflects for a moment before speaking.

Michael: You wouldn't have a dash of curaçao to go in the cognac, would you?

Winston: *(Ringing for Evans—doing a passable imitation of a Cork accent)* Was it not far from curaçao you were reared?

Michael: Yes, but *(doing a better imitation of Winston)* it is my mission to learn by experience.

Winston: In the category of alcoholic beverages, and their accompaniments, this representative of England can offer you anything you desire: without conditions and in a spirit of unrestricted open-handedness.

                (To Evans, who has quickly appeared) For Mr. Collins, a large Hine, with a tincture of curaçao.

Michael: Wait — you wouldn't have a Napoleon brandy, would you?

Winston: Of course. Anything you desire.

A momentary silence.

Winston: *(continuing)* Lady Lavery spoke to me about your early years in London. I understand you and she first met at the Court Theatre in Sloane Square before the Great War?

Michael: We did. She's — she's always taken a great interest in my doings. Even when I was a humble post office clerk here in London.

Winston: I think you were very successful in your work at the post office. As you have been everywhere, Mr. Collins. In your spare time, anyhow, from your commitment to the Irish Republican Brotherhood.

Michael: It might have been a fairer war if we had as much intelligence on ye, as ye have on us.

Winston: *(ignoring this point for the moment)* Lady Lavery speaks very well of you. I think she is rather smitten, you know. But then many of the London ladies are dazzled by your appearance, Mr. Collins.

Michael: *(sarcastic, codding)* Amn't I'm thinking of taking up a career in the Hollywood pictures by and by?

                Have you known Hazel Lavery — and her husband — for long?

Winston: Oh yes. Hazel is my painting instructor. She has taught me, better than anyone, how to wield a paintbrush. She gave me the assurance to do so. In times of desolation, most particularly, painting is my hobby.

Michael: She's been a good friend to Ireland.

Winston: A remarkable woman and a considerable beauty. A most talented painter too. I have just attended the opening of her new exhibition at the Alpine Gallery.

I was informed, at the soirée which followed, that you are sitting for a portrait by Sir John.

Michael: If I have the patience to compose myself. Sitting still is a torment.

The two are served with their drinks. Michael is given an amazingly large brandy glass, to which he mutters, "Jesus, Mary and Joseph". Evans disappears with some discretion.

Winston: You must regard yourself as honoured to sit for Sir John Lavery. The King and Queen, with the Prince of Wales, and Princess Mary, have been among his subjects. And remember, Sir John seeks to immortalise you.

Michael makes an impatient response, as though to dismiss the idea, murmuring "Yerra"… in the Munster manner.

Winston: *(continuing)* He has described you as — "a pasty-faced young Hercules". *(He lifts his glass)* To Sir John's endeavours.

Michael: And to Hazel's. She truly has been a devotee to the Irish cause — as well as a most affectionate friend to me.

Winston: Indeed. Where would you Irish patriots be without the beautiful and spirited women who have embraced the cause of Ireland — and her patriots?

Michael: *(in his own world, momentarily)* Ah, you know — she talks to all these Tory swells and tries to get them to see sense. Lord Londonderry. And of course Birkenhead — who, to my surprise, I like.

Though he did prosecute poor Roger Casement. And spread all those odious fucking lies about the man's private life.

Winston: I do not care for the notion of making a man's private failings into a public scandal.

Michael is about to launch into an argument about Roger Casement, but thinks better of it.

Winston: *(continuing)* I trust there is someone other than Lady Lavery awaiting you in Ireland. Some beguiling young colleen, perhaps, with marriage in mind?

Michael: I daresay, now, that your intelligence services are well able to inform you about my personal friendships.

Winston: I am not persuaded that they are. Consider — we couldn't even catch you when you were evading us, on your bicycle. When the popular press called you the Irish Pimpernel.

Michael: It didn't stop you putting a price on my head — of £5000. You hunted me day and night. I never slept two nights in the one bed.

Winston begins foraging in a drawer for something.

Michael: *(continuing)* And now I sometimes wonder what it was all for. When I was on the run, I knew what I was doing. Now, I'm not so sure.

A pause for thought

Michael: *(continuing)* Action is easier than politics. Clearer. Sometimes even cleaner. A lot of codology and bullshit bound up in politics.

After some more rummaging, Winston extracts what he has been searching for.

Winston: You see, Mr. Collins. I am no stranger to the experience of being hunted, myself.

(He holds up a tattered picture of himself when young, with the words "Wanted, Dead or Alive—£25—Gesoek: dood of lewendig! Vergoeding, vyf-en-twintig pond!" written in English and Afrikaans.)

Michael examines it, and is duly amused.

Michael: That's a nice bit of handiwork, to be sure! It's highly droll to think of yourself on the run from the gallant little Boers.

Winston: I was hunted day and night by the Boers.
But observe this closely: I was of much less value than you, Mr. Collins! For the price on my head was a mere £25. While you were sought for the sum of £5000.

Michael: Ah well, you'd have to take inflation into account.

He goes on looking at the Boer poster with interest.

Winston: It is a tribute to your people that no one betrayed you for the very considerable sum of £5000. One could purchase several fine farms in the golden vale of Tipperary for that amount.

Michael: Certain individuals must have been tempted, I'd say. But the people were behind us, for the most part. Our movement, Mr. Churchill, was *democratically* supported...

Winston: Are they behind you now?

Michael: They seem very enthusiastic. They're everywhere I go. I was nearly mobbed to death by young ones looking for my autograph at the Albert Hall the other night.

Winston: They are attracted by your heroic allure. But, more significantly, they are enthusiastic for a settlement, I think. They want peace. Everyone wants peace. As the Good Book says, there is a time of war, and a time of peace.

Michael: *(with a riposte to shows he knows the quotation).* A time to kill and a time to heal.

Winston: *(Melancholy)* A time to be born, and a time to die.
To every thing there is a season, and a time to every purpose under heaven.

Michael: Ah behind all this fine Biblical talk is *real politics*, though, isn't that it? Isn't that what you're saying? If we don't sign the Treaty, ye will go back to a time of war?

Winston: That is always a possibility. Indeed, that is always a possibility. *(A little threatening)* And a return to war would mean a real war this time — not mere bushranging.

Michael: Is that what you call the sacking of Cork, Mallow and Balbriggan, or the events of Bloody Sunday, when your forces opened fire on a football crowd — bushranging?

Winston: The Crown forces did not always distinguish themselves — but they were acting in reprisal. *(Unexpectedly, suddenly angry)* You had fourteen of our officers killed in their beds, some in the very presence of their wives, some at a moment of conjugal tenderness.

Michael: Don't think I wanted to do it! It made me sick every time I had to carry out a job. Sick, sick, sick.

Michael: *(continuing)* But how, otherwise, do we secure an independent Ireland that for generations upon generations — that my father himself, God rest his soul — lived for?

There are moments in life when the only choice you have is to fight! All these high-flown negotiations are all fine and dandy. But sometimes the only way to attain your objective is to fight for it! We wanted our freedom — we had to fight you for it!

Winston: Sometimes it is necessary to fight. Sometimes it is imperative. But just now — you do not have to fight any more. You have done the fighting.

Evans appears again, and refills their glasses silently but watchfully.

Evans: Will there be anything else, Sir?

Michael: Yes, William. Bring us up a 32-county Republic, would you?

Winston: Our Irish friends like "codding", Evans.

Evans: *(taking it all in)* Yes, Sir. *(He exits)*

Winston: *(holding up his drink)* Sláinte!

Michael: *(Correcting Winston's bad pronunciation)* Sláinte!

Winston: *(trying again, but no better)* Sláinte!

Michael: Hell of a good brandy.

Winston: For those who carry the heavy burden of office, I consider vintage brandy is a necessary perquisite of the job.

Michael: Pity ye aren't as generous in your terms as you are with your hospitality!

You know, I sometimes get the impression that you want to extract the last penny from us, and a penny after that again. You want control of our trade, our naval facilities, foreign affairs, our economy...

Winston: We can make progress on these issues, Michael...Look here, I know you want the prosperity of Ireland, and so do I.

Ireland is a poor country and deserves the chance of prosperity.

Michael: Don't you be telling me Ireland is poor! Didn't I have to leave the country to earn my living in London because the country was too poor to support me!

Winston: Mr. De Valera seems only to care for the romantic—and the symbolic—in his visionary patriotic fanaticism.

Michael: Now that's codology, Winston. Sure, what is the Oath of Allegiance but symbolism?

Winston: No. Not so. The Oath of Allegiance is about the defence of the Realm. Symbols are important. I know that. But for government, men must also have a practical vision. They must know how to do, not just how to dream.

I speak as one who has known failure in practical politics, and patriotic elation in fighting for my country.

Michael: I have a practical vision for Ireland. I was the Minister for Finance, even when I was on the bloody run.

Winston: Indeed. I know what funds you raised, for stocks and bonds. You are a very practical man. Indeed a most practical man. One of our intelligence agents described you as "an organising genius."

That's why we want you within the Empire. We want the best!

Michael gives Winston a withering look after mention of the Empire. Then he descends into a brooding silence for a few moments.

Winston: We…all want the prosperous Ireland that you care about…

Michael: I'm bloody depressed about all this, I don't mind telling you. I cannot see the end in sight. I was — or I tried to be — optimistic on the first days, little enough as I wanted to be here.

But now I cannot see *how we can do it.* I cannot see how Griffith and I are ever going to go back to Dublin with an agreement that will be acceptable. I just can't see it.…

Winston: I can, you know. I can. *(Suddenly very enthusiastic with his big idea…)*

You accept Dominion Status — that means an Irish Free State which would be on a par with Canada, with Australia, with South Africa. That is no mean status.

You have governance of your home affairs — but you take the Oath of Allegiance to the King — all right, an Oath of Allegiance to the King. Just to give us the security of knowing Ireland would not act seditiously towards the United Kingdom.

Ulster retains her Parliament, with the option of joining an all-Ireland Parliament in the future …

Michael: For Jesus' sake…

Winston: Hear me out — hear me out! — with active encouragement from London to join an all-Ireland Parliament in the immediate future.

Winston: *(continuing)* Perhaps within four or six years. I repeat—you will have charge of your domestic economy; but the Royal Navy must be able to defend the seas around the British Isles, and have access to all ports.

Michael's face looks like thunder.

Winston: You will have, in effect, an...an independent Ireland. *(He recoils from this phrase, but says it all the same.)* Within the limits of real politics.

Michael: It's not independence! It's Home Rule with knobs on! The Crown is giving away almost nothing!

Winston: *(With a sense of urgency)* Do you understand the political risks we have taken, Michael? We are on a very sticky wicket, in this Coalition.

We in the Liberal party could be signing our political death warrants by entering into a Treaty with Sinn Féin!

Michael: *(very quietly)* And I could be signing my actual death warrant.

Freeze. Darkness.

Interval

Scene Six

Winston and Michael as at the end of Scene Five.

Winston: *(With a sense of urgency)* Do you understand the political risks we have taken, Michael? We are on a very sticky wicket, in this Coalition.

We in the Liberal party could be signing our political death warrants by entering into a Treaty with Sinn Féin!

Michael: *(very quietly)* And I could be signing my actual death warrant.

A silence.

Evans knocks on the door discreetly and enters.

Evans: Mr. Churchill: Mrs. Churchill has telephoned from the country. She did not wish to disturb you by calling you to the telephone. She was pleased to be informed of the business in hand.

(He looks meaningfully towards Collins, and back to Winston.)

She assumes you will be writing to her tonight.

Winston: Thank you, William. My dear wife may rely upon my correspondence, as usual. Are the children all right?

Evans: She assured me that the children were in excellent form. *(Discreet cough)* Mr. Griffith and Lord Birkenhead are with the Prime Minister.

Winston: I am pleased to hear it. Serve them with the best we have.

Evans: The Prime Minister suggests that you and your guest might join them, presently.

Winston: We shall do that, William. After Mr. Collins and I have a little more time together.

Evans: Will there be anything else, Mr. Churchill, for you, or your guest?

Winston: Yes. You could bring us a bottle of champagne, William. The Pol Roger, of course. *(Evans assents and makes to go)* See if we have a 1911. *(Evans goes)*

Michael: Celebrations seem a bit premature. Not to say a bit fucking ridiculous.

Winston: Oh, bugger celebrations. This may be the only face-to-face meeting you and I ever have. I would like you to drink a vintage champagne with which to remember it.

Throughout my life, I have sometimes been short of financial means: but never so indigent that I was deprived of champagne.

Michael: *(mocking)* Or a fine Havana cigar rolled on the thigh of a Cuban maiden.

Winston: *(serious)* You are a young man, Michael Collins. You have your political career before you. I am a man of nearly fifty. I believe that Destiny does not intend me to live to be an old man. My father died at 46, and I have already outlived him by a year. And if this Government should collapse — and, I remind you yet again, it is teetering on the point of collapse — and the new Socialist Party should rise to power — my political career may well come to its termination, even before my life itself has faded.

Michael: Ah, sure it's all in God's hands. We must concentrate on the present. And do our best for today. *(He lifts his brandy glass and drains it)*

Winston: Indeed. Sufficient unto the day is the evil thereof. You may contemplate shooting a Bishop, Michael Collins, but you still trust in God! I like that immeasurably.

And I mean no disrespect when I say that this is charmingly Irish. *(Holds up his hand to prevent contradiction)* I intend no disrespect and, moreover, much affection.

Do you know that my earliest memories are of Ireland?

Michael: Huntin', shootin', fishin'…?…Ireland was a great recreation ground, wasn't it, for ye-all…

Winston: Ah—I was but a small child…Is it not strange that from the moment that my consciousness dawned—of being and dwelling upon this sceptred globe—that that consciousness was formed by Ireland?

Michael: You'll remember what your Duke of Wellington said about being born in Ireland: "One may be born in a stable without being a horse."

Winston: *(Musing)* I had a pleasing time in Ireland, with my beloved nurse, Mrs. Everest. I was two years of age. The year was 1876. My grandfather, the Duke of Marlborough was appointed the Viceroy by Mr. Disraeli.

Michael: You picked a bad time to come, by God. The 1870's were desperate. There was another famine threatening in Donegal. Mayo too. The people were starving…My father lived through all that. The horrors he witnessed…

Winston: Life entailed hardship for humble folk everywhere. Mrs. Everest often spoke to me of the poor people in Kent. We politicians must strive to ameliorate the hardships of the poor—which I have sought to do, with my social insurance reforms…

Winston: *(continuing)* However, in Ireland it was always raining, a circumstance which is but little amenable to amelioration.

Evans appears with the champagne, and pours some for both men.

Michael: *(Almost muttering to himself)* One generation succumbs to famine. The next to champagne and brandy.

Is this a form of decadence? Self-indulgence…?

Winston: *(continuing as though in a reverie)* The rain notwithstanding, my mother relished her many happy hours riding to hounds in the Irish countryside. My mother—who shone for me like the evening star, but at a distance—died this year.

Michael: Ah, I'm sorry for your trouble, Winston. My heartfelt condolences. Hard to lose a mother. A sorrowful event…

Winston: She died as she lived. Those that live by the sword, die by the sword. And those that live by the fashions of high society, perish by its vanities. She fell downstairs wearing a very fashionable pair of very high-heeled new Italian shoes, which she had recently purchased.

The accident caused a haemorrhage, and her pretty little leg had to be amputated just above the knee. She jested that she should now have to put her best foot forward. But, quite suddenly, she had a fever and died. She seemed so young at 67. The wine of life ran in her veins.

She was an American, you know.

Michael: Ah—that's why you think anything is possible. It's your American optimism…

Winston: Yes, she did appreciate her time in Ireland. She always said it was the best country in the world for horses.

Michael: I wouldn't quarrel with that. I'm fond of a horse myself. We had a lovely white mare when I was a child. Gipsey. I used to ride her bareback, holding on to her mane.

Winston: A horse! What a privileged childhood you had, Michael Collins! When I was a small child in Ireland, I merely had a donkey. Indeed, the donkey gave me my first introduction to Irish politics. I was out riding my donkey, aged three years, when we thought we espied a long procession of Fenians approaching us.

Michael: Ooohhh. *(makes a mocking boogey-man mime)*

The actors should gradually — only very gradually — begin to show signs of some inebriation. Both men hold their drink well, but nevertheless, they are consuming a fair amount of alcohol.

Winston: The donkey expressed his anxiety by kicking. I was thrown off, and suffered a concussion of the brain.

Michael: Did the ass knock sense about Irish politics into your head — or out of it?

Winston: You may have your jest, my dear friend, but the Irish donkey imperilled my young life very gravely. Without the tender attentions of dear Mrs. Everest, I might have been carried away, and I should not have been here, to support Mr. Lloyd George in his endeavours.

Or to support you in yours: which I mean to do. You would be faced with the tender mercies of Mr. Bonar Law, and his diehards.

Michael: You mightn't have been here to hang Kevin Barry either.

Winston: The Fenians were not figments of our imagination, you know. When I was but a small child, at the Vice-Regal Lodge in Dublin, I was given a toy drum by a man called Mr. Burke.

Winston: *(continuing)* Two years afterwards, when we had returned to England, Mr. Burke was quite suddenly murdered in the Phoenix Park—along with Lord Frederick Cavendish—by Fenian assailants. Everyone in England was very, very shocked. And so, I am told, were many people in Ireland.

Michael: The Fenians arose from the politics of despair. I think of my own father working out on the bogs and cutting the turf, and how hard he worked, living on the hope that one day we would have an Ireland, Gaelic and free.

Winston: Did you have an affectionate bond with your father, young Michael?

Michael: I'll tell you now, Winston. I lived in childish wonder of the man. He inspired me with complete trust: an implicit faith in his goodness and strength. If he told me, now, to jump out of that window over there, I'd have done it for him.

   When I was a gossoon, I'd follow him around our farm, whatever he was doing. I'd have followed him to the ends of the earth. Sure didn't he dote on me?

Winston listens wistfully.

Michael: My father was what you'd call a peasant farmer—that's what he was. Yet he was a man avid for reading. And learning. He knew Greek, Latin, French, Irish, of course. Men like my father, were held back by the terrible circumstances of Ireland's plight. He was the seventh son of a seventh son. Do you know what that signifies, Winston?

Winston: A lively and fertile marriage-bed...?

Michael: Ye know nothing over here of the life of the earth, of the people, of the folk traditions. A seventh son of a seventh son is a healer.

Winston: Splendid! Just what the world needs.

Michael: Ah, but as I say, Irishmen like my father were held back by the desperate circumstances of the country in the last century. If we'd had the opportunities we should have had, my father would have been something remarkable — a great scholar maybe.

To think of what he could have achieved — it doesn't make me bitter. Being bitter is no good. But it made me hard.

Winston: And yet, how fortunate you were to be in such a loving bond with your father. It was the small tragedy of my childhood that my father had little time for me. I sought to please him in every way: he was the greatest and most potent influence on my early life, and I had intense admiration for him. Yet I seldom talked with him, and never on terms of intimacy.

Michael pours more champagne for them both.

Winston: *(continuing)* I sometimes wished my father had been a man of humbler position. A skilled artisan — I might have been apprenticed to him. I used to watch the grocer's son, helping his father to arrange the front window of their small shop. To me, that seemed a bond of very great significance.

I mean to do better with my son. And you, Michael, no doubt you will repeat the happy relationship, with your sons, when you become a father.

Michael: Begod, I'd hope to embark on the role a little earlier than my Pa did. Wasn't he seventy-five years old when I was born!

Winston: *(with admiration)* Seventy-five! When he begot you? Superb! By heaven, if he'd stood for election, he'd have swept the country!

Michael: Ah, but then he died when I was only seven, in 1897. He'd been born, himself, back in 1815.

Winston: The year of Waterloo! That *is* romantic — to have such a direct link with history!

Michael: Yes. I needn't tell you — we sided with the French.

Winston: Of course you did! "England's difficulty is Ireland's opportunity."

Michael: I'll drink to that. *(He does)*

Winston: And that, my dear Michael, is *just* why we must have the allegiance of the new Irish State!
If we have another *difficulty* — with a troublesome Continental warlord — you might take another *opportunity*.

Michael: *(mock-sarcastic)* Oh Winston! How can you imagine such a thing?

Winston: But you have just made an avowal that your sympathies were with the French when Bonaparte threatened our country. The Irish have an instinct to disoblige England. Thus, you must be able to comprehend how an independent Irish Republic could be a threat to Great Britain?

Michael: Winston — you've got this arseways. It's not Ireland that's a threat to England. It's England that's always been such an almighty fucking threat to Ireland!

Winston: Ah, *'the great Gaels of Ireland/The men whom God made mad...'*

Michael: *'...For all their wars were merry/And all their songs were sad.'* Chesterton.

Winston: You know, my father had some affection for Ireland, whatever people might say. He believed in the education of the people. And in religious tolerance.

Michael, thinking of Lord Randolph, looks sceptical but he makes no rejoinder to this. He has understood Winston's yearning to be loyal to his father.

Winston: Alas, there are many subjects on which we shall never agree.

Michael: Well, we can agree on G.K. Chesterton. Have you read *The Napoleon of Notting Hill?*

Winston: Oh, capital! And *Lepanto.*

Together: 'Love-light of Spain — hurrah!
Death-light of Africa!
Don John of Austria
Is riding to the sea.'

Mild cheers

Michael: How does it go, now…Let me see…
'The cold Queen of England is looking in the glass;
The shadow of the Valois is yawning at the Mass…'

Together: 'From evening isles fantastical rings faint the Spanish gun,
And the Lord upon the Golden Horn is laughing in the sun.
Dim drums throbbing, in the hills half heard…'

They lose the thread…then Michael starts again…

Michael: 'Where only on a nameless throne a crownless prince has stirred…'
Something, something, something. Then — 'Strong gongs groaning as the guns boom far/Don John of Austria is going to the war…'

Together: 'Stiff flags straining in the night-blasts cold
In the gloom black-purple, in the glint old-gold
Torchlight crimson on the copper kettle-drums
Then the tuckets, then the trumpets, then the cannon, and he comes…'

Winston: Excellent stuff. They don't write 'em like that any more. *(Looking gloomy)* Not after the Armageddon of Flanders, they don't.

Michael: I love that line — 'Stiff flags straining in the night-blasts cold/In the gloom black-purple, in the glint old-gold.' It conjures up the whole Mediaeval battle-field, in all its magnificence.
Battle poetry is inspiring. I love it.

Winston is sunk in reflection for a moment.

Michael: C'mere to me, you'll know this one.
'Half a league, half a league, half a league onwards
All in the valley of death/Rode the six hundred
Forward, the Light Brigade!
"Charge for the guns!" he said
Into the valley of death/Rode the six hundred.'

Together: 'Cannon to right of them/Cannon to left of them.
Cannon in front of them/Volleyed and thundered'

Brief pause to think of next line

'Stormed at with shot and shell —
Boldly they rode and well —
Into the jaws of Death/Into the mouth of Hell
Rode the six hundred.'

Winston: An unforgettable description of a total balls-up.

Michael: *(now in his stride)* 'Forward, the Light Brigade!
Was there a man dismayed?
Not though the soldier knew
Someone had blundered.'

Together: 'Theirs not to make reply
Theirs not to reason why
Theirs but to do and die
Into the Valley of Death
Rode the Six Hundred.'

Michael: *(a little maudlin)* 'Theirs not to reason why/Theirs but to do and die...' I sometimes think that's the mission that Dublin has sent me on.

Winston: Oh yes, commanders do blunder. By God, they do. But the Irish are a warrior race, my dear Michael. Always were. Always will be.

Michael: The Four Masters of Ireland used to say that every Irishman is born a soldier or a monk. And I'm no bloody monk.

Winston: Aha! But you go to Holy Mass at Brompton Oratory every morning, just the same!

Michael: Are your bloody spies still following me around? Call off the dogs of war, would you! Small wonder I don't trust any of ye.

Winston: Oh, I know you don't trust me, my dear Michael. You wrote it down yourself.

Winston: *(continuing)*
(Takes a note from his pocket and reads rather dramatically...)
'Will sacrifice all for political gain… Inclined to be bombastic. Full of ex-officer jingo or similar outlook. Don't actually trust him.'
Mr. Collins' confidential assessment of Mr. Churchill.

Michael recognises his own words describing Winston Churchill…

Michael: Well, wasn't I right—haven't you used your bloody spies to get hold of the confidential note itself!

Winston: Yet we have to establish trust. It's the only way we can ever go forward. It's the only way to put an end to the hatreds that have flowed between Ireland and England.

Michael takes up a child's soft toy lying on the ground, and turns it over in his hands.

Winston: And see how intermingled England and Ireland are. We speak the same language. We know the same recitations, the same poetry.

Michael: I speak a language you don't know. And there's a lot of poetry I'd know that you wouldn't have a clue about. I only gave you my English recitations, not my Irish ones. Out of diplomatic…considerations. And I wouldn't know any of your Eton Boating Songs.

Winston: Harrow, if you please!
(He takes a watch from his waistcoat and looks at it) Another before we join Mr. Griffith, along with Lloyd George and F.E.?

Michael: I've had enough champagne, thanks.

Winston: A self-disciplined man who sticks to his limits.

Michael: No, I mean I'd prefer to go back to the brandy and curaçao.

Drinks are poured again...

Winston: That's better. I have little liking for these puritans who seek to curb us from drinking, smoking, eating, from pleasure...

Some of those unflinching Suffragettes were of this cast of mind. Temperance campaigners! Heaven forfend!

For a moment they resemble a couple of boozers propping up a bar...

Michael: Women in politics! I can think of better places for them.

We have a couple of terrible harridans among our female republicans! Mary MacSwiney. Constance Markievicz. They want every man to die for Ireland: and none to live for it.

Winston: *(Holds up his glass)* To the ladies! God bless 'em — and keep 'em out of Parliament!

Michael: The ladies! Where would we be without them! *(Long pause)*

No, I can't deny it, Winston. I cannot deny it. Women have been good to me, all the same, and, sure, I love them all.

Winston: *(An attempt to be "Irish")* And sure, why wouldn't you, and they all falling over you...

Michael: Still and all, when all this is over — when we have the governance of Ireland, as is our right, Winston: as is our democratic right — I'll get married to Kitty — who's faithful waiting for me while I philander beyond in London with society hostesses...*(a touch sarcastic)*.

Winston: A wife is a great comfort in life, Michael. Mark my words. A wife is a **great** comfort in life. *(Emotional)*

Michael: *(Looking at the toy in his hands)* Fortunate is the man who has a good wife, Winston. Fortunate is that man. And children. Children are a great blessing. Didn't my father have eight? And you should see De Valera's brood. They're lovely little creatures altogether. It's the best thing about the long hoor. *(Pause)* I didn't say that. *(Salutes)* Dev is my commander. No, his children really are most beguiling — I'm killed playing with them.

And yours, Winston. Sure your children must be grand, too. Whose is this toy, now, for example?

Winston: It has been the plaything of all my children.

Michael: How many do you have now?

Winston: We are fortunate to have a dear daughter aged 12, Diana. A most cherished son, Randolph, aged ten. And a dear little girl of seven, Sarah. They are all splendid children. Splendid children. *(A pause)* Our beloved Marigold died in August this year. She was two and a half.

Michael: Died — at two and a half? Ah, the poor little thing. That's desperately sad altogether.

Winston: By Jove, I blubbed a good deal over that, I confess.

I've seen men die in atrocious conditions in battle. I've heard Henry Wilson dismiss the death of a thousand men as "a small setback". Yes — I have signed execution orders, though never with an easy heart. And yet, the death of this adored little child affected me as deeply as anything I've ever known.

It was — that her little life had only just begun. And seemed so full of promise for the future...

Michael looks genuinely sad.

Winston: *(continuing)* She was in the charge of a young French governess when she developed a sore throat and then septicaemia. The governess was tardy in summoning a doctor, or to telegraph for my wife. By the time we arrived by her bedside…

He tails off…a pause.

Winston: *(continuing)* She had a sweet little singing voice, and she loved the popular song — "I'm forever blowing bubbles." Do you know it?

Michael: I've heard it. 'Twas heard a lot this year.

Winston: *(he sings it in a "diseur" voice: but the music itself may be heard as a distant echo)*

'I'm forever blowing bubbles,

Pretty bubbles in the air.

They fly so high, nearly reach the sky,

Then like my dreams they fade and die.

Oh, fortune's always hiding,

I've looked everywhere where.

I'm forever blowing bubbles,

Pretty bubbles in the air.'

Winston: Clementine was sitting with her and suddenly the child said, 'Sing me Bubbles…' On the following day she died. *(He is distressed. There is another pause)* We called her The Duckadilly. *(Pause)* I blub very easily.

Michael puts his arm around Winston and gives him a rough hug.

Michael: God knows, you have reason to weep. Sure, tis the worst thing in the world, to see a young child die. The worst thing in the world.

(He seems to be recalling something of what he has seen)

Winston: *(Recovering himself)* Yes. It was a painful and heavy loss. My wife was distraught with grief. The poor little Duckadilly.

Another echo of the Bubbles song…

Michael: *(Pacing about)* Did you change your mind about pursuing the war in Ireland because of your own sorrows?

Winston: It has occurred to me that it may have had some bearing upon it. I was certainly pressed to alter my approaches by Clementine. Oh… it was a confluence of many things.

Michael: You could have gone on fighting us, you know. You could have. We couldn't have held out for more than another week.

Winston: Physically, we could have continued. But not morally. The world was turning against us. Your American campaigns bore fruit.

Michael: America—that was Dev's doing. He knew how to rouse the Americans in Ireland's favour. And do you think, Winston, morally, that you could now go back to war?

Winston: *(not quite wanting to show his hand)* Mm…A time to kill and a time to heal…
You may have given me your English recitations, but you haven't yet heard my Irish recitation—which I learned when I was a very young child in Ireland…

Michael: Go on, then. I'm all ears.

Winston: *(declaims dramatically, slurring slightly)*
'The Harp that once through Tara's hills
The soul of music shed
Now hangs as mute on Tara's walls
As if that soul were fled.'

Winston: *(continuing)* 'So sleeps the pride of former days,
          So glory's thrill is o'er
          And hearts, that once beat high for praise,
          Now feels that pulse no more!'

Michael commences the second verse, and they both say it together:
          'No more to chiefs and ladies bright
          The harp of Tara swells:
          The chord, alone, that breaks at night,
          Its tale of ruin tells.'

          'Thus Freedom now so seldom wakes
          The only throb she gives,
          Is when some heart indignant breaks,
          To shew that she still lives!'

Winston: *(lifting his glass sentimentally)* Érin Go Bragh!

Michael smiles a sad smile, reflecting for a moment..

He then leans forward with a serious, and suddenly sober, air.

Michael: Winston, if you can deliver the North of Ireland, we can come to some kind of a compromise on the vexed question of *allegiance.*

Winston: *(after a pause)* I'll tell you the truth, Michael. No one can deliver Northern Ireland. But we could use our best offices to persuade the Ulstermen to come to a reasonable settlement — *if* we stay in office.

Michael: At a pinch, I could accept the Empire. For the moment. As would Griffith. We could probably carry the others — all except Childers. His loyalty is to Dev.

He is pacing up and down now.

Michael: *(continuing)* But—we could work out some form of words—in which we were accepting of the British Commonwealth of nations—and the King as its head.

The British Empire won't last forever. Empires never do.

Winston: It would much sadden me to think upon its dissolution.

Michael: Ah, but *real politics*, remember! We sometimes have to face them...

If Arthur Griffith and I can convince the Dáil, and the Irish people, can you convince Belfast?

Winston: *(muttering)* Belfast doesn't want a Treaty, Michael. Belfast wants another Cromwell!

Michael: For Christ's sake, you have the power! Exercise it! Ah, we'll wrest the North-East of Ireland off you in the fullness of time anyhow...

Winston: I repeat my point, Michael. You in southern Ireland do not understand —you cannot force Ulster's hand, without a civil war that would destroy Ireland!

Michael: In all morality, we should at least have Fermanagh and Tyrone!

Winston: Ah, Fermanagh and Tyrone! Those dreary steeples which rise again after every cataclysm the world has passed through.

(Pause while thinking)

What we could do is appoint a Boundary Commission to arbitrate on who obtains Fermanagh and Tyrone. And we could set up a Council of Ireland which would meet regularly. And we could recommend to Belfast that it join an all-Ireland Parliament...

Michael: Well. It would be the freedom to achieve freedom.

Winston: We can never have wholehearted agreement. You and I know that. But if you trust me, I will support the Irish Free State. *Coûte que coûte.*

Michael takes Winston's hands. For good measure, he gives him a thump on the shoulder.

Michael: All right, Winston. I trust you. I trust you not to let me down.

They shake hands.

Evans appears at the door. Darkness. Music: "I'm Forever Blowing Bubbles."

Scene Seven

Again the Newsboys: the younger one is carrying his news satchel. The older one is behind a newspaper stall. They are shouting their usual wares: "Standard, Star, News." "Express, Mail, Telegraph, Morning Post." Younger boy is also carrying an advertising bill with the message:

December 6: DAILY EXPRESS "Treaty Signed: New Irish Free State."

Older newsboy puts up a bill poster:

THE TIMES – IRISH SETTLEMENT – WORLD-WIDE SATISFACTION. THE KING'S JOY.

(Sub-titles) **"Wide powers for the Irish Parliament or Dáil Eireann."**

Their voices fade and we hear the voice of Florence Fitzgerald, reporting to the copytaker —

Florence: There was general rejoicing yesterday at the news that the Government and Sinn Féin had signed a Treaty of peace between Great Britain and Ireland.

The whole world acclaims Mr. Lloyd George as a peacemaker, but the twelve men who set their names to the Treaty also bore the heat of the day. Lord Birkenhead and Mr. Arthur Griffith, Mr Winston Churchill and Mr. Michael Collins brilliantly brought the final stages of a sometimes difficult negotiation to a successful conclusion…

A new Irish Free State is to come into existence: it will have the same status as the Dominion of Canada. Members of the Irish Parliament will take an oath of allegiance to the King, which also includes an oath of allegiance to the new Free State. After five years, Ireland may undertake her own coastal defence, with her own navy.

Ulster may stay out of the Irish Free State for as long as she please but should she remain out, a Boundary Commission will readjust her borders. It is expected that the King will open the new Irish Parliament.

Backdrop pictures of Dublin.

Florence: *(continuing)* Scenes of elation are reported from Dublin. Princess Mary will be welcomed in the near future to Portumna, in Co. Galway,   the Irish castle belonging to Lord Lascelles, which, although recently unfortunately burned down, will forthwith be restored…

As her voice tails off, the older newsboy comes on stage with a fresh bill poster bill poster:

December 8: DAILY TELEGRAPH "Sinn Féin Bombshell: De Valera to Reject the Anglo-Irish Treaty."

A boom sound as scene fades.

Then darkness to indicate the passage of time…

Scene Eight

*Evans, alone in Winston's library. He is walking around, arranging and tidyi
Evans has the slightly fusspot manner of a butler; but he is shrewd, intelligent a
watchful...*

Evans:	Mr. Churchill is a peculiar type of man.
	No consideration whatsoever for his staff and servants.
	Calls you at any time of the day or night. Can't do anything himself. Can't run his own bath. Can't tie his own shoelaces.
	Yet we'd all go to the ends of the earth for Winston.
	He's a man of many contradictions, see. He loved soldiering, a yet he's really very sentimental.
	He feels strongly about certain things—the sainted Brit Empire is one of them—but he has a kind of valour towards opponents.
	He fought hell-for-leather against the South African Boers; l afterwards he proclaimed them *(imitating Winston)* "a gall enemy".
Evans:	(continuing) He was dead set against the Irish when they had t rebellion in 1916, in the middle of the Great War. He called th every kind of murderer. I heard him tell Mrs. Churchill that Irish had a "vicious, unreliable streak in their character".
Pause	
	But something happened to him in 1921. And after that...he v a man of war who wanted to make peace.
Pause	
	He's very soft on his children. Calls them pet names. Never sma them. He loves being a father. He never had much mothering fathering himself, see.

Evans: *(continuing)* And once he signed that Treaty with the Irish, it was as if the whole Irish situation became his personal child.

Michael Collins, who he had denounced as a gangster and a terrorist, became a young man of great concern for Mr. Churchill.

Think about this: he *worried* about Mick Collins. I saw one of Winston's letters to General Collins, as he then became. "Take care of yourself," he wrote at the end, kind of protective-like. 'The times are very dangerous.'

I never knew him to say that to any other man. "Take care of yourself."

More business with tidying-up.

Evans: *(continuing)* Winston would use these fatherly expressions about the Irish situation in general. You know — he talked about "nursing" the Irish Free State through "a difficult birth". Like it was his personal commitment to midwife that Irish legislation through the House of Commons.

It was his political responsibility, all right. He was the Colonial Secretary, and he was in charge of all the Dominions and Ireland was now a Dominion.

Like Canada — only not really like Canada. Because of Ireland, Winston had to sleep with a revolver under his pillow, as he was a known target for assassination.

When did anyone have to sleep with a revolver under his pillow because of Canada? Yet far from upsetting him, the danger seemed to ginger him up. I think he really liked the excitement of it.

Pause

Politically, things here were on the edge, from the start of 1922. Lloyd George's Coalition was losing ground, and the Conservatives were playing silly buggers.

In Ireland itself, all hell was breaking loose. The Irish parliament voted for the Treaty that Mr. Collins and Mr. Griffith brought back from London all right. The people and the Catholic church — a power to be reckoned with in Ireland — were all in favour.

Evans: *(continuing)* But you had all this disagreement from the ultra-revolutionaries who wanted a full-blown Republic, and nothing but a Republic, and no Oath of Allegiance to the King. There was a feminist firebrand called Countess Markiewicz who called for the shooting of Michael Collins for compromising with the English. "If no man is man enough to do it," she says, "I'll do it myself!" Oh…*(he shakes his head disapprovingly)*. I wouldn't like to have one of those at home!

So a civil war broke out between the Irish who were pro-Treaty and those who were anti-Treaty…And then there was a lot of trouble in the North of Ireland. Oh, by God, yes. When is there not?

Pause. More business with arranging books, etc.

Evans: *(continuing)* Mr. Churchill had a very trying time in the House of Commons when he was transferring the Crown Powers to the Irish Provisional Government.

There was a lot of this "nursing" going on. He provided the Free State with hardware, yes: with arms and tanks. He was that committed to bringing the Irish Free State to birth. And he was that committed to Michael Collins.

Evans: The Conservative Diehards, with the Unionists, of course, gave him hell. They brayed and barracked and taunted. They proclaimed that Ireland was falling into disarray and chaos: they urged him to send British troops to re-occupy the country.

Evans momentarily fades. Backdrop picture of the House of Commons and general noise of Parliamentary debate.

Voice No 1: Mr. Churchill is pursuing a policy which is absolutely futile! The Crown forces should have the freedom to pursue military operations in the Free State, which is swiftly descending into lawlessness once again!

Cries of Hear! Hear!

Voice No 2: In Ulster a ruthless campaign is being waged by our enemies against the Loyalist people. The Rt. Hon. Gentleman will tell me that Mr. Collins has nothing to do with them, but I gravely doubt that. The Unionists in Southern Ireland are being killed without mercy, their property destroyed, and they are being run out of the country!

Voice No. 3: We have withdrawn the British troops. We have disbanded the Royal Irish Constabulary. We have handed over Dublin Castle and all that it stands for. We have given a political amnesty to the Sinn Féin prisoners: we have given the Free State Government £1,500,00 and a full call on rates and taxes with which to carry on their administration. But Mr. Collins has not been able to honour the Treaty which he and Mr. Griffith signed! How can Mr. Churchill justify this disgraceful turn of events?

Voice No. 4: How long are we going to go down this slippery slope and allow Civil War in Ireland? How long can the Colonial Secretary defend this situation?

More parliamentary noise and baying... Gradually fading.

Lights up on Evans as before.

Evans: *(continuing)* Actually, it wasn't just the diehards. Even some of the liberal Home Rulers attacked Winston, holding him responsible for the disturbances in Ireland. He stood there, you know, battling valiantly, defending the creation of the Irish Free State — and the leadership of Michael Collins — against this cacophony of hostile voices.

I was there, myself, on an errand, on the worst day. So was General Collins. He had to come back to London on several occasions, to talk to Sir James Craig, and Winston.

On this particular day in May, Michael Collins was observing the debate from the Distinguished Strangers' Gallery. Winston was standing on the floor of the Commons — the butt of this baying Parliamentary mob, you might say, all shouting against him.

As though through a veil, we see an outline of Michael Collins, now in military uniform, sitting high up in the Distinguished Strangers' Gallery of the House of Commons, watching a debate on the floor intently.

We then see Winston, on the floor of the Commons, looking up at Collins meaningfully.

Evans: *(continuing: sonorously)* My governor then looked up, and he saw Michael Collins above in the Strangers Gallery. And you know…

A pause

…there passed between them a certain look.

We see Winston and Michael exchanging a look of complicity.

Evans: *(continuing)* I don't know, how, quite how to explain it—It was a look of trust. It was as though there was a certain—an allegiance between them.

When General Collins seemed at his most despondent during the meetings they had to have together in that summer of 1922, Winston tried to reassure him with an old phrase he'd picked up in the Transvaal. "Alles zal regt kom."

"Alles sal regt kom." That means—"All will come right", you know.

Evans looks at Winston's set of toy soldiers.

Blackout. Music. "A Nation Once Again." (Lyrical, not martial)

Scene Nine.

This is a scene without words. A picture of Michael Collins appears on a screen, and a shot is fired. Blood appears on the picture, courses down it slowly, and it falls to the ground.

Music. "A Nation Once Again": very sombre. Darkness. A silence.

Scene Ten

We return to the first scene of Churchill dictating his recollection of the period.

Winston: The presentiment of death had been upon Michael Collins for some time; from that moment when he signed our Treaty. In all my life, I have never seen so much passion and suffering in restraint as I saw on Michael's face on that day. Yet he knew that this Treaty was the best that could have been agreed in the circumstances. We could not go an inch further than we did.

Pause.

The shadow of death did not restrain his courage or impair his sense of mission. When he met with the fatal ambush, his second in command, urged him to drive on: it was characteristic of Collins that he riposted – "No: let's stop and fight them."

Before he died Michael Collins sent me a valedictory message. "Tell Winston we could never have done it without him." I valued that. I valued that a good deal.

Pause.

Winston: *(continuing)* As I anticipated, the Liberal Coalition of Lloyd George dissolved that very year of 1922, and the whole composition of British politics altered.

The Labour party displaced the Liberals, and I soon found myself without a party, without a seat, and, after a sudden operation without an appendix.

Pause and smile.

But the Almighty greatly consoled us when a new, beautiful baby daughter Mary was born to us.

Everything had changed, in England as in Ireland: except the ever changeless Fermanagh and Tyrone. The Boundary Commission fell into desuetude.

Winston: *(continuing)* We lost office—perhaps in my case, forever. And the promises made to Mick Collins—that we would use our best offices to persuade Northern Ireland to enter into an all-Ireland settlement were never fulfilled.

Pause.

Heroes are more apt to be flawed men than paragons of perfection. For all that, Michael Collins supplied those qualities of action and personality without which the foundation of the Irish nation would never have been established. And I came to support the conviction that it should be established.

A long pause. Winston goes over to window, takes out a cigar and gazes into distance.

Winston: *(continuing)* This was the poem I meant to recite to him—
                 'For how can man die better
                 Than facing fearful odds
                 For the ashes of his fathers
                 And the temples of his gods.'

Slow fade. Picture of Collins in increasing close-up. Music: "If I Had a Talking Picture of You.

Ends

Appendix I

Churchill and Collins: descriptions of their characters from historical sources, for the use of actors, and students.

Michael

In those hot and troubled days Collins was in a real sense of the word a heroic and romantic figure. There was about him something more romantic than fewness of years. Mr. Chesterton once sang of the Gaels that come from Ireland that they are 'the men that God made mad — For all their wars are merry /And all their songs are sad.'

If Collins did not impress one as a man of song, he looked at all events a man of high heart who would wage a merry war. He had the masterly physique that young men love in a hero. His body was big and burly, and the massive head, set squarely on broad shoulders, was adorned with plentiful hair as black as the traditional raven's wing. When he was in a temper, which was rarely, his eyes flashed and his hand contracted its restless, prehensile fingers into a mighty fist that hammered emphasis into his words with blows like a smith's anvil beats. He sat always in the Dáil at Arthur Griffith's side, with the air of a very large nephew being protective to a shy, small uncle.

Next to his power of giving and claiming affection, one thinks of his boundless energy. He did not speak; he shouted. He did not walk; he bounded. He emphasised his words not with a nod or a wink but with a tremendous shake of the head that brought his black mane tumbling down over his dark eyes. And then the hand, at once strong and nervous, would be pushing it back again. It is harder to think of that abounding vitality being cut off suddenly than it is to think of the passing of Arthur Griffith or Cathal Brugha. How they are passing, those who in the winter nights fought over the body of Ireland!

But always one comes back to Collins as Irishmen think of him — the affectionate man — Mick Collins. Strange how there have been marriages as well as deaths among the Irish leaders recently — quite a number of them. Nobody knew anything about them till they had taken place. But everyone knew that Mick

Collins was engaged. Those were the sort of things people did know about him the homely, affectionate things that touch us all.

The Manchester Guardian: Thursday, August 24, 1922 *(editorial after the news Collins' death).*

✿

Michael Collins was thirty-one years of age—a typical Irishman, if ever the was one. He was tall, massively built and weighed fourteen stone. His appearance was striking. His features were handsome, and his forehead was crowned with thick crop of dark brown hair. His eyes twinkled when he spoke, and his voice had a soft Irish brogue. When he laughed, his whole frame shook. Impulsive generous, brave to the point of recklessness, his was a legend in the Republican movement...His hair-breadth escapes were numerous.

Though he lived in Dublin and had his headquarters there, he was never caught A reward of £10,000 [this is an exaggeration] was offered by the authoriti for his arrest, but riding on an old bicycle, he bore a charmed life. On sever occasions the house where he was reported to be staying was surrounded by th police, only to find that he had escaped a few minutes earlier. On one occasio when the police entered the hotel where he was reported to be, they found the t half-drunk in a tea-cup and still hot. Collins had escaped to the roof, clambere along the rooftops of adjoining houses, jumped through a skylight of anoth house, and got away.

Sir Geoffrey Shakespeare (PPS to Lloyd George in 1921): *Let Candles be Broug In.* (1949)

✿

When I try to recall my first meeting with Collins, the principal thing that strik me is how rapidly and completely I found myself on terms of the greatest intima with him. He was at the time slim and equally boyish in appearance and manne hardly looking his 25 years. I was first impressed by his frank friendliness, h infectious gaiety and rollicking high spirits. He held at the moment no position authority, his manner was free from pretentiousness, and no occasion had arise to call forth a display of his extraordinary qualities of intellect and character. B even at this stage he displayed his genius for making friends, and attaching me to himself by the strongest bands of affection; and, after a very short time, those new friends whom he had made...had become strongly attached to him...

His face was intensely mobile and expressive, changing rapidly from a scowl of anger to a broad grin of enjoyment, now showing scorn or defiance and now the sunniest good humour. His restless energy showed itself in a series of abrupt jerky movements, and in an explosive brusquerie of manner which often offended the pompous and pretentious, and those sedate persons who disliked hurry. He always dressed well, and was particularly neat and tidy in his habits. His suits were generally of dark grey. In winter he usually wore only a light raincoat; I do not remember ever seeing him in a greatcoat, nor in any form of headgear except a soft hat...He was a moderate drinker...though on a few occasions, he took brandy with curaçao...

Piaras Beaslai: *Michael Collins and the Making of a New Ireland.* (1923)

Winston

My father [H.H. Asquith] and his friends were mostly scholars, steeped in the classical tradition, deeply imbued with academic knowledge, erudition and experience. Their intellectual granaries held the harvests of the past...In certain fields of thought there was to them nothing new under the sun. But to Winston Churchill everything under the sun was new — seen and appraised as on the first day of creation. His approach to life was full of ardour and surprise. Even the eternal verities appeared to him to be an exciting personal discovery. And because they were so new to him he made them shine for me with a new meaning. However familiar his conclusion it had not been reached by any beaten track. His mind had found its own way everywhere.

Again — unlike the scholars — he was intellectually quite uninhibited and unselfconscious. Nothing to him was trite. The whole world of thought was virgin soil...Nor was he afraid of using splendid language. Even as I listened glowing and vibrating to his words, I knew that many of my captious and astringent friends would label them as "bombast", "rhetoric", "heroics". But I also knew with certainty that if they did they would be wrong. There was nothing false, inflated, artificial in his eloquence. It was his natural idiom. His world was built and fashioned on heroic lines. He spoke its language...

Action or speech transformed him. The clay became a mobile and translucent mask through which his inner being shone, transfusing it with light and fire. I then assumed an infinite variety of Protean shapes—in turn that of an orator a pugilist, a statesman, or a Puckish schoolboy cocking defiant snooks at authority. Every emotion was faithfully reflected. His was a face that could no keep a secret. His personality thrust its way through so forcibly that his feature seemed irrelevant trappings of his intrinsic self...

His mind contained no insulating dodges or devices, no fireproof curtains watertight compartments. Once engaged by a theme it was wholly possessed.
Violet Bonham Carter: *Winston Churchill as I Knew Him.*(1965)

He is a typical child of his time. It is a time of feverish activity, of upheaval and challenge, of a world in revolt...Into this vast turmoil, Mr Churchill plunge with the joy of a man who has found his natural element. A world in transition is a world made for him. Life is a succession of splendid sensations, of thrilling experiences. He rushes from booth to booth with the delight of a boy at a fa And each booth is more wonderful than any other...He is reckless of his life an of his money, indifferent to consequences...

With this abnormal thirst for sensation, he combines an unusual melodramat instinct. He is always unconsciously playing a part—an heroic part. And F is himself his most astonished spectator. He sees himself moving through th smoke of battle—triumphant, terrible, his brow clothed with thunder, his legion looking to him for victory and not looking in vain. He thinks of Napoleon; F thinks of his great ancestor...in that fervid and picturesque imagination there a always great deeds afoot with himself cast by destiny in the Agamemnon rol Hence that portentous gravity that sits on his youthful shoulders so oddly, tho impressive postures and tremendous silences, the body flung wearily in the chai the head resting gloomily in the hand, the abstracted look, the knitted brow... His mind once seized with an idea works with enormous velocity round intensifies it, enlarges it, makes it shadow the whole sky. In the theatre of tha mind it is always the hour of fate and the crack of doom.
It is this impressionableness that makes him so vital and various...

Brilliantly as he preaches, he is the man of action simply, the soldier of fortune, who lives for adventures, loves the fight more than the cause, more even than his ambition of his life…

His appearance and his utterance are against him. There is still no better pen picture of him than that which the Boers issued in the warrant for his arrest after his escape from Pretoria: "Englishman, twenty-five years old, about 5ft. 8in. high, indifferent build, walks with a bend forward, pale appearance, red-brownish hair, small moustache hardly perceptible, talks through the nose and cannot pronounce the letter 's' properly." It is not a flattering picture. That defect of speech alone would have destroyed most men. Mr Churchill makes you forget it by the sheer energy of his mind and manner.

A.G. Gardiner: *The Pillars of Society* (London 1916)

Winston started in politics as a Tory – a Tory Democrat of the school founded by his father, Lord Randolph Churchill. He criticised his leaders, quarrelled with them, attacked them and crossed the floor of the House to join their opponents, the Liberals. There for some years he associated with the Radical wing, and supported them in urging a reduction of naval expenditure…He served as a Coalition Liberal under Lloyd George, but when the Coalition fell, he drifted away from the party and called himself a Constitutionalist, under which title he rejoined the Tories. Later on, however, he challenged his leader, Baldwin, on the India question and slid into the position of an independent Tory critic of the substantially Tory government.

These changes of side are facts of his history. When they were thrown up at him once in the House, he blandly retorted: "To improve is to change. To be perfect is to have changed often." ….The fact is that Winston is not, in the accepted sense, a good party man. He will not swallow and digest the policies thrust on him by any party. Always he must choose and decide for himself. His party has but one member—Winston Churchill.

Malcolm Thomson: *The Life and Times of Winston Churchill.* (1940)

Bibliography.

Beaslai, Piaras. *Michael Collins and the Making of a New Ireland.* Dublin 1923

Bonham Carter, Violet. *Winston Churchill as I Knew Him.* London 1965

Bourke, Richard. *Peace in Ireland: The War of Ideas.* Dublin 2003

Bromage, Mary C. *Churchill and Ireland.* University of Notre Dame Press, 1964.

Churchill, Winston S. *The World Crisis: The Aftermath* London 1929

Churchill, Winston S. *Thoughts and Adventure:* London 1932

Churchill, Winston S. *My Early Life.* London 1944

Coogan, Tim Pat. *Michael Collins* London 1990

Coote, Colin R. (Ed). *Sir Winston Churchill – a Self-Portrait.* London 1954

Doherty, Gabriel & Keogh, Dermot (Eds). *Michael Collins and the Making of the Irish State.* Dublin 1998

Forester, Margery. *Michael Collins: The Lost Leader.* London 1971

Foster, Roy. *Modern Ireland 1600-1972.* London 1988

Foster, Roy. *Paddy and Mr Punch: Connections in English and Irish History.* London 1993

Gilbert, Martin. *Churchill – a Life.* London 1991

Gilbert, Martin. *Churchill – a Photographic Portrait* London 1974

Longford, Frank. *Peace by Ordeal: The Negotiation of the Anglo-Irish Treaty, 1921.* London 1935

Mackay, James. *Michael Collins: A Life.* London 1996

Manchester, William. *The Last Lion: Winston Spencer Churchill. Visions of Glory 1874-1932.* London 1983

Middlemas, Keith (ed). Thomas Jones: *Whitehall Diary*. Oxford 1971. *Vol.III – Ireland 1918-25*

O'Hegarty, P.S. *The Victory of Sinn Fein. Dublin 1924.* (Republished 1998)

McCoole, Sinead. *Hazel – a Life of Lady Lavery*. Dublin 1996

O Broin, Leon. *Michael Collins*. Dublin 1980

Osborne, Chrissy. *Michael Collins Himself.* Cork, 2003

Rhodes James, Robert. *Churchill – a Study in Failure: 1900-1939*. London 1970

Ryle Dwyer, T. *Big Fellow, Long Fellow – a Joint Biography of Collins and De Valera*. Dublin 1999

Shakespeare, Sir Geoffrey. *Let Candles be Brought In*. London 1949

Soames, Mary. *Clementine Churchill* London 2002

Talbot, Hayden. *Michael Collins – His Own Story*. London 1923

Thomson, Malcolm. *The Life and Times of Winston Churchill*. London, 1940

Salvidge, Stanley. *Salvidge of Liverpool: Behind the Political Scene*. London 1934

Williams, Desmond (Ed) *The Irish Struggle 1916-1926*. London 1966

The Times, the Irish Times, the Irish Independent

The Daily Express

The Manchester Guardian

The Morning Post

Hansard: *House of Commons Parliamentary Reports*